C
973.049 BAR
Barr, Lind-

Wm-ng r ad
j urne o
MOSQ 1074

WORN SON E

D0397766

Long Road to Freedom

Journey of the Hmong

by Linda Barr

Reading Consultant:
Timothy Rasinski, Ph.D.
Professor of Reading Education
Kent State University

Content Consultant:
Dr. Mark Bender
Assistant Professor
Department of East Asian
Languages and Literatures
The Ohio State University

Red Brick™ Learning

Published by Red Brick™ Learning
7825 Telegraph Road, Bloomington, Minnesota 55438
http://www.redbricklearning.com

Copyright © 2005 Red Brick™ Learning. All rights reserved.

Library of Congress Cataloging-in-Publication Data
Barr, Linda, 1944–
    Long road to freedom: journey of the Hmong / by Linda Barr.
    p. cm.—(High five reading)
    Includes bibliographical references (p. 62) and index.
    ISBN 0-7368-3880-5 (hc)—ISBN 0-7368-3852-X (pbk.)
    1. Hmong Americans—History—Juvenile literature. 2. Hmong (Asian
people)—History—Juvenile literature. 3. Refugees—United
States—History—Juvenile literature. 4. Refugees—Asia,
Southeastern—History—Juvenile literature. 5. Vietnamese Conflict,
1961–1975—Hmong (Asian people)—Juvenile literature. I. Title. II. Series.
E184.H55B37 2004
973'.0495942—dc22
                             2004003558

Created by Kent Publishing Services, Inc.
Executive Editor: Robbie Butler
Designed by Signature Design Group, Inc.
Edited by Jerry Ruff, Managing Editor, Red Brick™ Learning
Red Brick™ Learning Editorial Director: Mary Lindeen

This publisher has made every effort to trace ownership of all copyrighted
material and to secure necessary permissions. In the event of any questions
arising as to the use of any material, the publisher, while expressing regret for
any inadvertent error, will be happy to make necessary corrections.

Photo Credits:
Cover, pages 48, 50, Gerald Cubitt; pages 4, 8, 11, Bettmann/Corbis; page 13,
Alinari Archives/Corbis; page 14, Brian Vikander, Vikander Photography; page
16, AA WorldTravel Library; page 19, Steve Raymer, Corbis; pages 22, 26, 41,
43 (bottom), 47, Mark Downey, Lucid Images; page 24, Hulton-Getty; pages 17,
27, 29, 36, Michael S. Yamashita, Corbis; page 30, Lindsay Hebberd, Corbis;
page 31, Marianne Henderson, Third Rock Images; page 32, Atlas Geographic;
pages 35, 43 (top), Doranne Jacobson, International Images; page 51, Art
Directors; pages 53, 54, Alison Wright, Alison Wright Photography

No part of this book may be reproduced without written permission from the
publisher. The publisher takes no responsibility for the use of any of the materials
or methods described in this book, nor for the products thereof.

Printed in the United States of America.

1 2 3 4 5 6 09 08 07 06 05 04

Table of Contents

— CHAPTER 1 —
Caught in a War

"Toukee, Kao, run quickly!" Toua Chang shouted at his two older children. Then he pushed his wife and 3-year-old son, Teng, ahead of him. They were just outside their village, racing into the jungle in the hills of Laos.

China

North Vietnam

Laos

Thailand   South
            Vietnam

Cambodia

A long stream of people flee their villages to the safety of the jungles of Laos.

Trying to Escape

Toukee (TOO-kee) was 12, and Kao (KOW) was only 8 when their family fled from the Communist soldiers. The children could barely hear their father over the explosion of gunfire. Bullets whistled around them.

It was 1972. Communist soldiers were shooting at Toua (TOO-ah) Chang and other Hmong (MONG) men as they fled their village. These Hmong men had helped U.S. troops fight the Communists in Laos during the Vietnam War (1954–1975). The soldiers wanted revenge. If women and children got in the way, they died, too.

Some say Hmong means "free people," but the Hmong have had a long struggle to be free. The Vietnam War was not the first time the Hmong had to flee for their lives.

---

flee: to run away quickly
Communist: a person who believes in Communism, which is a system where the way of producing goods is owned and shared by the community
revenge: to do harm or evil in return for harm or evil that has been done

The Long Search for Freedom

The Hmong story begins at least 5,000 years ago. Ancient legends say the Hmong once lived in a cold land north of China.

These ancient Hmong had grown crops on the same land for many years. Few minerals remained in the soil. So they moved to the nearest land that had not yet been farmed. The Hmong cleared this land so they could plant their crops.

ancient: of times long ago
legend: a story about real events handed down through the years, but probably not entirely true
mineral: a substance formed in the earth

Forced to Move

Some time later, the legends say, the Hmong were forced to move farther south. After moving many times, the Hmong finally migrated to southwest China.

Later, native Chinese also moved to southwest China. The Hmong were forced deep into the mountains. They left good farming soil along the river plains. Some Hmong worked for the Chinese, who often treated the Hmong workers badly. The Chinese forced the Hmong to pay high taxes. The government used Hmong workers like slaves to build roads and complete other projects.

Often, the Chinese did not allow the Hmong to follow their own customs or speak their own language. Sometimes they stole Hmong land and burned their villages. Many Hmong fought back and were killed.

---

migrate: to move from one place to another
native: born or belonging in a certain place
custom: something that has been done for a long time

Yet Another Move

Though many Hmong moved deeper into the mountains, some began to leave China. They moved south to Vietnam, Laos, and Thailand. But governments in these countries, too, would not allow the Hmong to be free.

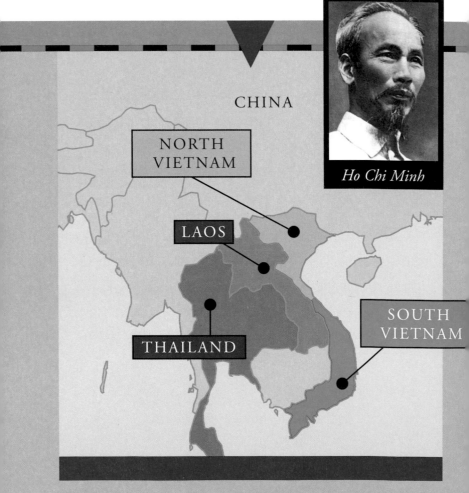

CHINA

NORTH VIETNAM

LAOS

THAILAND

SOUTH VIETNAM

Ho Chi Minh

War in Vietnam

In 1945, France controlled Vietnam. The Communists in Vietnam wanted control of the country, however. So they began to fight the French. The leader of the Communists was a Vietnamese man named Ho Chi Minh (hoh chee MIN).

In 1954, to end the fighting, France, several other countries, and leaders of the Communists signed an agreement in Geneva, Switzerland. The agreement split Vietnam in two. North Vietnam became Communist. South Vietnam became democratic.

In the late 1950s, Ho Chi Minh tried to take control of South Vietnam. The United States worried that the Communists would try to take over other countries in Southeast Asia as well. The U.S. government sent troops to fight the Communists. This conflict became known as the Vietnam War.

---

democratic: having to do with a government ruled by the people
Southeast Asia: a part of Asia that includes the countries of Vietnam, Laos, Cambodia, Thailand, Malaysia, and Indonesia

The War Spreads

In the early 1960s, the Vietnam War spread to nearby Laos. Ho Chi Minh sent troops and supplies from North Vietnam through Laos to reach the fighting in South Vietnam. To stop this, the U.S. Central Intelligence Agency (CIA) organized a secret army in Laos. The CIA trained thousands of Hmong men and boys as soldiers. These Hmong soldiers would help the U.S. troops stop Ho Chi Minh's supplies and troops from reaching South Vietnam.

A Difficult Choice

Many Hmong in Laos believed they had to help the Americans. These Hmong thought it was the only way they would ever be free. The CIA promised to help the Hmong after the war. Some other Hmong didn't want to help the United States, however. They chose to join the North Vietnamese forces.

Central Intelligence Agency (CIA): a branch of the U.S. government that spies on other countries

Many Hmong soldiers were just boys.

Helping the U.S. Troops

The secret Hmong army in Laos worked alongside the U.S. troops. Together, they fought the Communists.

The Hmong helped the U.S. troops in many ways. They stole supplies that were sent from North Vietnam to the Communist soldiers in Laos and South Vietnam. They rescued American pilots when their planes crashed. Thousands of Hmong soldiers fighting in Laos died during this time.

The American people did not know about this secret army. They would not find out about it for many years, until the Hmong would need help from the United States.

Lives Changed Forever

The Vietnam War lasted from 1954 to 1975. During those years, Laos, Vietnam, Thailand, and the Hmong culture were changed forever.

But how had the Hmong lived before the Vietnam War? The next chapter describes the quiet Hmong way of life—before the soldiers came.

Hmong women dressed in traditional clothing, around 1955

— CHAPTER **2** —

Life before the War

Kao hurried behind her brother as they raced into the jungle. As she ran, she glanced back at her small village. Before the war, their lives had been simple. Who would look after their fields now? Who would take care of their water buffalo? When would they see their small farm again?

A Hmong village in Laos

A Farming People

Before the war, the Changs had lived like many other Hmong families in Laos, Thailand, and Vietnam. Their home was a hut made of wood and bamboo, with a roof of palm leaves. The hut had a dirt floor and no running water. The Changs cooked their meals over a fire outside the hut.

Huts were often crowded. A husband, his wife, or wives, and their unmarried children lived in one large hut. Often, married children built huts close by their parents' and grandparents' huts.

The Changs, like most Hmong families, were farmers. They planted rice and corn, along with other vegetables and fruits. Some families also kept cows, pigs, horses, and water buffalo. Some raised fish in lakes and flooded rice paddies.

---

bamboo: a lightweight wood
paddy: a flooded field where rice is grown

Clearing Land

For centuries, the Hmong had used the same methods to grow their crops. In January, the men and boys cleared the fields. Hmong farmers cleared new fields by cutting down trees and burning them. This practice, over many years, had destroyed much of the forest in Laos and Vietnam.

Hmong farmers cleared much of the forest in Laos and Vietnam.

Planting Rice

In May, the women and children weeded the fields. Then they used sticks to poke holes in the soil. They dropped several grains of rice into each hole. Later, rice plants sprouted and grew.

Each field was weeded twice more during the summer. In the fall, the women cut and dried the long stalks of rice. Then they beat the stalks to break off the rice grains. Next, they put the grains into baskets and threw the rice into the air. This was so the wind could blow away the dirt. Finally, they pounded the rice to remove the husks.

A Hmong girl cleans rice.

stalk: the main stem of a tall plant
husk: the hard outside covering of grain

Farming on a Mountainside

Often there was not enough land in the valleys to grow food for everyone. So the people planted rice paddies and cornfields high on the mountainsides.

To do this, families first dug away soil on the mountainside to make flat areas for planting. Then they built low walls to keep the soil and water from sliding down the mountain.

Some Hmong walked hours each way to get to their fields in the mountains. Many carried plants, their harvested crops, and other supplies in large baskets that they wove themselves.

Hmong children carry supplies in large, woven baskets.

Everyone Must Work

Life was not easy for the Hmong, even before the war. Everyone in the family had to work, from early in the morning until late at night. Both men and women worked in the fields. Nearly all the work was done by hand. Some farmers had water buffalo to pull their plows through the muddy rice paddies.

Little Time for School

Before the war, few Hmong children attended school. They were too busy working in the fields, preparing food for the family, or taking care of younger brothers and sisters.

Sometimes a father sent a son to school for a few years. The school was often in another village. It could take hours to walk there, so students lived at school during the week. They walked home on weekends to help on the family farm.

The Fruits of War

The Hmong led a simple life. They were a farming people. They grew rice in paddies. They planted corn and kept cows, pigs, horses, and water buffalo. They had lived this way for centuries.

The Vietnam War changed this way of life. It forced the Hmong to make tough choices—join the side of the United States, or join the side of the Communists. Some Hmong tried to stay out of the fighting. They just wanted to be safe. But no matter what they chose, their lives changed forever.

Like the Changs, many Hmong fled into the jungle, leaving their farms behind. But life in the jungle had its own dangers. What do you think these were? Where could the Hmong finally find safety and true freedom?

— CHAPTER **3** —

From the Jungle to the Camps

Kao could still hear the Communist soldiers shooting at the fleeing families. Despite the danger, she stopped running and cried, "Father! Where is Father?"

"The Communist soldiers took him!" Toukee whispered in horror. "I saw them!"

"Come with me!" their mother whispered. "We'll be safe in the jungle."

This storycloth shows the Hmong living in the jungle.

Life in the Jungle

Life in the jungle was very difficult for Kao, Toukee, Teng, and their mother. There was little food. Sometimes, Toukee caught birds and other small animals to cook and eat. Mostly, the family ate berries, fruits, and roots.

Many Hmong died of starvation and illness. But they had nowhere else to go. If the Communist soldiers found them, they would imprison them, or worse.

The Changs and other Hmong families hid in the jungle for years. Many hoped to return to their farms and villages when the war was over. For many, that dream would never come true.

---

starvation: the condition of not having enough food to eat
imprison: to put or keep in prison

The War Ends

After years of fighting, the United States lost the Vietnam War. In 1975, U.S. troops withdrew from Vietnam and Laos. They left behind the secret army of Hmong soldiers.

As soon as the U.S. troops withdrew, the Communists took over South Vietnam and Laos. The Hmong who had fought for the Communists were safe. The Hmong who had fought against the Communists were now in great danger.

Communist soldiers often burned the villages of the Hmong who fought on the side of the United States.

The Killing Continues

The Communist soldiers hunted down members of the Hmong secret army. They killed them and their families. Now there were no U.S. troops to protect the Hmong. Communist planes dropped bombs on Hmong villages. Communist soldiers set fire to the jungle with napalm (NAY-palm). Many thousands of Hmong soldiers and civilians, including children, died.

Some Hmong surrendered to the Communists, who then treated them as slave workers. Many Hmong would not live as slaves, however. They decided to leave Laos. They hoped to find freedom in a new land.

---

napalm: a substance that can be shot or dropped on an enemy and set on fire
civilian: someone who is not in the armed forces
surrender: to give yourself up

Crossing the Mekong River

To escape from Laos, thousands of Hmong fled across the Mekong (MAY-kahn) River. On the other side of the river was Thailand. There, they would be safe from the Communist soldiers. Many families walked for days just to reach the river.

At the river, they were met with more danger. There was no bridge for the Hmong to cross. A few people had boats, and some tried to swim across the rushing waters. Others clung to rafts made from bamboo poles or banana leaves. It could take three hours or longer to cross!

This storycloth shows the Hmong crossing the Mekong River.

Death in the Water

On the Laos shore of the Mekong, Communist soldiers kept watch. They searched the waters for people trying to escape from Laos. They shot anyone they spotted. Often, dead bodies floated on the river.

The fast-moving Mekong River separates Laos from Thailand.

The Refugee Camps

From 1975 until 1990, hundreds of thousands of Hmong fled Laos. No one knows for sure how many tried to escape. Most who made it went to Thailand and were placed into refugee camps there.

One of the largest of these camps was named Ban Vinai (bahn ve-NYE). The United Nations operated this camp. At one time, more than 45,000 Hmong lived in Ban Vinai. About half of them were children.

Ban Vinai was better than most camps. It had a market, health clinic, school, lake, and soccer field. Refugees could study English and work on nearby farms.

---

refugee camp: a camp created for refugees, who are people who flee a country in search of a safer place
United Nations: an organization of nations that works for world peace

*Two Hmong women carry supplies at the
Ban Vinai refugee camp.*

Living Conditions

Most refugees at the camps lived in rows of bamboo barracks. The barracks had dirt floors and straw roofs. As many as 10 families lived in each barrack. Sometimes, up to 200 people shared one bathroom.

Some families had space for a little garden, so they grew food for themselves. But many had to depend on the camp to give them food.

This family is cooking over an open fire in a refugee camp.

barrack: a building that looks like a shed or a barn and is used to house people for a short time

Family Is Important

In the camps, the Hmong tried to follow their customs and traditions. Family is very important to the Hmong. When possible, they lived as before, in groups or clans. Before the war, as many as four generations of one clan might live together.

This woman's colorful clothing shows that she belongs to the Flower Hmong Clan.

clan: a group of people who are related to each other
generation: all the people born around the same time

The color of cloth worn on their heads shows which clan these Hmong belong to.

The Hmong Clans

The main Hmong clans from Laos and Thailand were the Green Hmong and the Armband Hmong. The main clans from Vietnam included the White Hmong, Blue Hmong, Black Hmong, and Flower Hmong.

When possible, the Hmong wore hand-woven clothing that showed which clan they belonged to. Most camp refugees, however, had to wear whatever clothing they had.

No Written Language

The Hmong wanted to record their experiences of the war and of life in the jungle and in the camps. However, they had no written language.

Legends say that long ago in China, the Hmong had a written language. Sadly, this language was lost over time. Later, some Western missionaries tried to create a Hmong alphabet. Some Hmong women stitched these alphabet symbols onto their clothes. Years later, however, no one could remember what the symbols meant.

How could the Hmong in the refugee camps preserve their history? Without a written language, they needed to find a different way.

---

missionary: a person sent out by a religious group to teach that group's beliefs and do good works

symbol: an object, mark, or sign that stands for something

The Storycloths

The Hmong began to record their history on storycloths. Hmong women had always been skillful at needlework. They used this skill to create pictures of their experiences. Sometimes men drew pictures showing the events that happened in their lives. Then the women embroidered these pictures onto cloth.

These storycloths helped trace the history of the Hmong people. For example, some storycloths showed the Hmong fleeing into the jungles of Laos. Some showed them crossing the Mekong River and entering the refugee camps.

Relief workers from other nations bought some of the storycloths and sent them to their home countries. For example, some American workers sent storycloths back to the United States.

---

embroider: to stitch designs on cloth using a needle and thread
relief worker: someone who tries to help people, especially refugees

The storycloths helped the Hmong preserve their history and share it with others. In addition, selling the cloths earned money for the Hmong, who needed it badly.

Creating the storycloths also gave the refugees something to do as they waited to leave the camps. Most hoped to go to the United States. America, they thought, was a land of freedom and prosperity. What hardships might also await the Hmong in America? How might life change for the Hmong in America—for better or worse?

This storycloth shows traditional village life.

---

prosperity: the condition of being successful or wealthy
await: to wait for something or someone

CHAPTER 4

Moving to America

"Toukee, please come with us to the United States!" Toukee's mother begged. "We have spent four years in the camp waiting for this chance!"

A Hmong girl waits for permission to leave the Ban Vinai refugee camp.

Time to Go or Time to Stay?

Some Hmong decided to stay in Thailand. Toukee, now 19, had met Mai (MYE), age 16. Mai was another refugee. They were going to be married and hoped someday to go back to Laos and farm the land again.

For Mrs. Chang, nothing was as it should be. Her husband, Toua, should have arranged Toukee's marriage. But Toua was still missing. The family should not be divided. But now some would go to America, and others would stay behind.

Mrs. Chang guided Kao, now 15, and Teng, 10, toward a bus that would take them to the airport. Soon, they would be on their way to begin a new life in the United States. Maybe this life would bring them freedom and safety at last.

Refugees and Immigrants

People move to another country for several reasons. Immigrants *choose* to leave their homes. They hope to find a better life in another country.

Refugees, however, *must* leave their home country. They are likely to be killed or put in prison if they stay. The Hmong were refugees.

Making Decisions

Some Hmong from the camps went back to Laos to try to farm the land. Some went back to fight the Communists. Some, like Toukee, stayed in Thailand. Like Toukee, they also hoped to return to Laos someday, but only when they could be safe there again.

Leaving the Camps

Most of the refugees wanted to leave Thailand, but not to return to Laos. Some traveled to Australia, France, and other countries. Most came to the United States.

First, though, they had to get permission from the United States to enter the country. To do this, families had to prove that they had supported the U.S. troops. However, many families had destroyed any proof that they had helped the Americans. They had not wanted the Communist soldiers to find this proof. This was one reason some families were not allowed to come to the United States.

Families who were not allowed to come to the United States or other countries were sent to several resettlement villages in Laos. Life in these villages was hard. The soil was poor, and crops did not grow well. Refugees in these villages were often hungry.

---

resettlement village: a place where Hmong refugees were sent to live

An Unknown Land

Thousands of Hmong refugees entered the United States in the 1970s. But before coming, many of them spent several months at Phanat Nikhom (FA-naht NEE-kom). This was a special camp in Thailand. At this camp, workers taught refugees a few words in English. The workers also taught the Hmong a little about what to expect in the United States. Many refugees did not even know where the United States was.

From Phanat Nikhom, the Hmong rode buses to the airport. Then they flew to the United States.

By 1990, more than 100,000 Hmong had entered the United States. Large groups settled in California, Minnesota, and Wisconsin.

A Hmong family living in Sacramento, California, 1987

Culture Shock

When the Hmong refugees arrived in the United States, most of them could speak, write, and read little or no English. They had never used a modern bathroom or turned on a water faucet. Now, they lived in high-rise apartments in strange cities.

Many Hmong had never ridden in a car. Very few knew how to drive. Many of the older Hmong boys had been soldiers. Now they were sitting in American high schools. How do you think they felt?

Even the Hmong's farming skills were of little use. They had no money to buy land and did not understand modern farming methods. Soon, many Hmong families ended up on welfare.

---

welfare: aid that a government gives to people who are poor

In Laos and Thailand, the Hmong traveled by water buffalo.

In the United States, the Hmong traveled by car or bus for the first time.

The Young Hmong Adapt

By the early 1980s, many Americans had learned about the Hmong. They knew the Hmong had suffered and many had died because they supported the U.S. troops.

Groups of Americans reached out to the Hmong refugees. The Americans helped them adapt to their new home.

Soon many younger refugees had learned English. They entered schools and did well—sometimes better than students who had grown up in the United States! The Hmong families strongly supported their children.

Some of the young refugees—both men and women—went on to college. They took classes in computer science, medicine, law, and education. They started their own businesses. These refugees no longer needed welfare. They had good jobs.

---

adapt: to change yourself because you are in a new situation

The Older Hmong Struggle

Many of the young Hmong who came to the United States had been born in the jungle or the camps. They had not seen the horrors of war—or they barely remembered them. They were ready to make a fresh beginning in a new land.

For many older Hmong, however, living in the United States was difficult. They had once been farmers. Then came the war. They had seen much suffering as they fought to survive. Next came the struggle to protect their families in the jungle, and then the camps. The older Hmong had many memories—hard memories. Now they faced still another challenge—finding their place in a new, modern land.

New Roles

The older Hmong women did not know what was expected of them in the United States. In their homeland, they took care of their families. They carried out the decisions made by their husbands, fathers, and fathers-in-law. The women knew they were supposed to serve others.

However, American society expected women to make decisions and learn new skills. Many older Hmong women felt overwhelmed in America.

Older Hmong men were better able to continue their traditional roles in the United States. They took charge and solved problems. However, some had low-paying jobs or no jobs at all. The men, too, struggled to adjust to this country.

---

overwhelmed: helpless
traditional: having to do with customs or beliefs that have been handed down

Lost in America?

In the United States today, many Hmong have adapted well. Others, however, continue to struggle. This is especially true of some elderly Hmong. These elders no longer have a strong role in their own culture. Many feel useless and lost.

What do you think it would be like to suddenly move to another country? Would it be harder for you or for your parents and grandparents to adjust? What would you have to do to adjust to your new home?

The days can be long and lonely for elderly Hmong living in the United States.

CHAPTER 5

Going Home

The Changs had lived in Minnesota for more than 20 years. Now all three of them were going back to Laos for a visit. Mrs. Chang had wanted to go back for many years. She secretly hoped they would find her husband there. She also longed to see her son, Toukee.

In Laos and Thailand, many Hmong still live as their families have for hundreds of years.

Together Again

Kao, now a lawyer, had arranged her family's trip back to Laos. She, Teng, and Mrs. Chang would travel together. Mrs. Chang lived with Teng. Teng would leave his wife and two daughters at home to run their small grocery store.

After the Changs arrived in Laos, a taxi took them close to the village where Toukee and Mai lived. The Changs had to finish the trip on foot, walking along a rutted dirt path. The journey was difficult for Mrs. Chang, now an elderly woman. When they reached the village, they saw that little had changed since the Communists took over. The villagers were living much as they had for centuries.

Finally, Toukee ran out of a small hut to greet them. Mai and their four teenage children were close behind him.

---

rutted: full of grooves and uneven

A Wish to Return

Every year, about 10,000 Hmong-Americans visit Laos, Thailand, and Vietnam. A few Hmong visit China. They want to learn more about their history. They also want to visit relatives who stayed behind after the Vietnam War.

Some of these travelers were infants when they left their homeland for the United States. Some lost both parents during the war, but they still hope to meet other relatives. Few, however, go back to Southeast Asia to live.

Today, visitors to Thailand can visit Hmong villages.

A Hmong child works in the fields of Vietnam.

The Struggle Continues

Today, life is still hard in Southeast Asia. Many Hmong live in huts and farm as they have for centuries. They must work hard. Many children do not go to school. Instead, they help in the fields.

Living on Tourism

A growing number of Hmong in Southeast Asia make their living from tourism. The tourists include former refugees who return to visit Southeast Asia. Many Americans who served in the Vietnam War want to see this area again, too. Other people come to enjoy the tropical climate.

Hmong guides take visitors on tours. The marketplace is one popular stop. There, tourists can buy many kinds of embroidered clothing. Jewelry, baskets, and other handmade items are also for sale.

Hmong Celebrations

Tourists also want to see Hmong celebrations, such as their New Year celebration held at the end of each calendar year. Many Hmong in the United States also celebrate the New Year. For the Hmong, this is a time of rest from the harvest and work. It is also a time of new beginnings.

---

tourism: an industry that provides places for travelers to stay and guides them on tours

On this holiday, the Hmong dress in handmade clothes. They ask the household spirits to help them in their daily lives. They beg the harmful spirits to stay away.

There is also singing and dancing. Musicians play bamboo flutes, two-stringed violins, cymbals, gongs, drums, and trumpets. They also play an instrument made from water buffalo horns.

This woman is dressed for the Hmong New Year's celebration.

This Hmong mother combines the old and the new. She is using a sewing machine to create an ancient pattern.

The Hmong's Long Journey

The Hmong people once lived in the mountains of China. Now they are spread around the world. Most are now adapting well to their new cultures. But some, especially the elderly, struggle to fit in and to live with sometimes painful memories.

The Hmong in the United States are far from their homeland, but they are trying to preserve their culture. Many teach their children ancient traditions, customs, and skills.

The Hmong paid dearly for supporting U.S. troops in the Vietnam War. How can the Hmong today best honor the culture, and the courage, of their ancestors? What can others do to respect and honor the Hmong?

---

ancestor: someone who comes earlier in a family line

Epilogue

More about the Hmong

The Hmong live all over the United States. The largest group lives in California. Many of these Hmong live in Fresno.

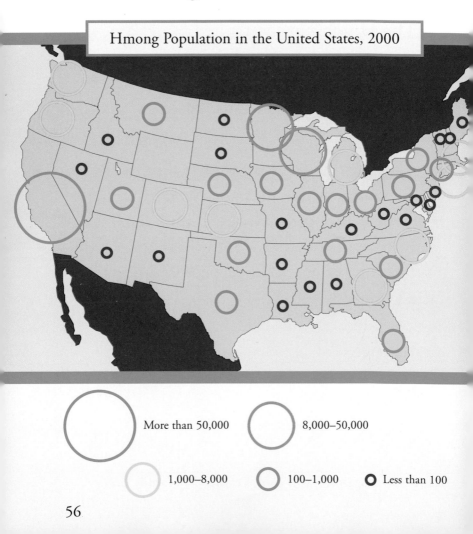

Hmong Population in the United States, 2000

More than 50,000

8,000–50,000

1,000–8,000

100–1,000

Less than 100

Marriage

In Southeast Asia, most Hmong marry between the ages of 14 and 18. A man may have more than one wife. Fathers used to choose their children's mates. Now many Hmong young people choose their own husbands or wives.

Religious Beliefs

Many Hmong-Americans are Christians. Most Hmong in Southeast Asia follow the beliefs of animism. They believe that spirits live in the earth, in the sky, in animals, and in people. Their spiritual leaders are called *shamans*. Shamans guide the Hmong through hard times and help heal the sick.

Honoring the Dead

Many Hmong set up an altar in their home to show respect for their dead relatives. They believe that the living and the dead are connected.

A Hmong Legend

Long ago, two men visited the seashore. They spotted a crane sitting on a nest of eggs. The men were hungry, so when the crane flew away to find food, they stole her eggs. They put a hole in each egg and emptied it out. After eating the insides, they put the shells back in the crane's nest.

The crane returned and saw her empty eggs. Being a special crane, she was able to fill them with a special powder. When she left again, the men took the powder. They put some of it on dead insects. Instantly, the insects came back to life.

The two men hurried to their village. Their chief had just died, but they put some of the powder on him. He came back to life! From that time on, the two men traveled from village to village, bringing the dead back to life. The thankful villagers gave them many presents.

Finally, the two men returned to their own village. They had not realized that their wives and children had died years before. They tried to bring them back to life, but their bones were too dry. The men were so upset that they threw their special powder away. They wanted to die, too.

The villagers begged the men not to leave them. However, the men said that after they died, a spirit would come to some of the people. The spirit would teach these people how to help those who were sick. These healers were to be called *shamans*.

Since then, shamans have helped the Hmong overcome sickness and hardship.

Glossary

adapt: to change yourself because you are in a new situation

ancestor: someone who comes earlier in a family line

ancient: of times long ago

await: to wait for something or someone

bamboo: a lightweight wood

barrack: a building that looks like a shed or a barn and is used to house people for a short time

Central Intelligence Agency (CIA): a branch of the U.S. government that spies on other countries

civilian: someone who is not in the armed forces

clan: a group of people who are related to each other

Communist: a person who believes in Communism, which is a system where the way of producing goods is owned and shared by the community

custom: something that has been done for a long time

democratic: having to do with a government ruled by the people

embroider: to stitch designs on cloth using a needle and thread

flee: to run away quickly

generation: all the people born around the same time

husk: the hard outside covering of grain

imprison: to put or keep in prison

legend: a story about real events handed down through the years, but probably not entirely true

migrate: to move from one place to another

mineral: a substance formed in the earth

missionary: a person sent out by a religious group to teach that group's beliefs and do good works

napalm: a substance that can be shot or dropped on an
    enemy and set on fire

native: born or belonging in a certain place

overwhelmed: helpless

paddy: a flooded field where rice is grown

prosperity: the condition of being successful or wealthy

refugee camp: a camp created for refugees, who are people
    who flee a country in search of a safer place

relief worker: someone who tries to help people,
    especially refugees

resettlement village: a place where Hmong
    refugees were sent to live

revenge: to do harm or evil in return for harm or evil
    that has been done

rutted: full of grooves and uneven

Southeast Asia: a part of Asia that includes the countries
    of Vietnam, Laos, Cambodia, Thailand, Malaysia,
    and Indonesia

stalk: the main stem of a tall plant

starvation: the condition of not having enough food to eat

surrender: to give yourself up

symbol: an object, mark, or sign that stands for something

tourism: an industry that provides places for travelers to
    stay and guides them on tours

traditional: having to do with customs or beliefs that
    have been handed down

United Nations: an organization of nations that works
    for world peace

welfare: aid that a government gives to people who are poor

Bibliography

Cha, Dia. *Dia's Story Cloth: Hmong People's Journey of Freedom*. New York: Lee & Low Books, 1996.

Jouanah: A Hmong Cinderella, adapted by Jewell Reinhart Coburn with Tzexa Cherta Lee. Arcadia, Calif.: Shen's Books, 1996.

Millett, Sandra. *The Hmong of Southeast Asia*. First Peoples. Minneapolis: Lerner Publications, 2002.

Murphy, Nora. *A Hmong Family*. Journey between Two Worlds. Minneapolis: Lerner Publications, 1997.

Shea, Pegi Deitz. *The Whispering Cloth: A Refugee's Story*. Honesdale, Penn.: Caroline House, Boyds Mills Press, 1995.

Useful Addresses

Hmong American Community, Inc.
1044 Fulton Mall, #207
Fresno, CA 93721

Hmong Cultural Center, Inc.
995 University Avenue West, Suite 214
Saint Paul, MN 55104-4796

Hmong National Development, Inc.
1112 16th Street NW, Suite 110
Washington, D.C. 20036

Internet Sites

**Information about Hmong Language
and Culture**
http://ww2.saturn.stpaul.k12.mn.us/hmong/
sathmong.html

Lao Family Community of Minnesota
http://www.laofamily.org/index.html

Index

1074539626